THE SPIRITUAL COUPLETS
OF
MAULANA JALALU-'D-DIN
MUHAMMAD RUMI

Abridged and Translated

E.H. Whinfield

Masnavi
Book 2

[ZHINGOORA BOOKS]

PROLOGUE.

THE Composition of this Masnavi has been delayed for a
season; 1
Time is needed for blood to become milk.
Till thy fortune comes forth as a new-born babe,
Blood becomes not milk, sweet and pleasant to the mind.
When that light of God, Husamu-'d-Din
Turned his course down from the summit of heaven,
While he had ascended to sublimest verities,
In the absence of his spring the buds blossomed not,
But when out of that sea he came to shore,
The lute of the poesy of the Masnavi sounded again.
This Masnavi, which is the polisher of spirits,
Its recommencement occurred on the day of "Opening."
The commencement date of this precious work
Was the year six hundred and sixty-two of the Flight.
The Bulbul started on this date and became a hawk;
Yea, a hawk to hunt out these mysteries.
May the wrist of the King be the resting-place of this hawk,
And may this door be open to the people for ever!
*NOTES:
1. The delay was caused by the grief of Husam for the
death of his wife.

STORY I.

The Sufi's Beast

After anecdotes of the man, in the time of 'Omar, who mistook his eyelash for the new moon, of one who stole a snake and got bitten by it, and of 'Isa's foolish disciple who besought the Lord to teach him the spell whereby he raised the dead, comes the following story.

A certain Sufi, after a long day's journey, arrived at a monastery, where he put up for the night, and strictly enjoined his servant to groom his ass carefully and give him plenty of litter and fodder. The servant assured him that his minute directions were superfluous, and promised to attend to the ass most carefully; but when his master's back was turned he neglected the ass, and the poor animal remained all night without water or food. Consequently he was weak and unfit to travel next morning, and in spite of the blows and kicks that were showered on him, could not carry his master, but had to be led. The other Sufis who were traveling with his owner thought that the ass was useless, and when they arrived at the place where they halted for the night, they sold the ass to a traveler, and with the proceeds of the sale bought delicate viands and torches, and made a feast. The owner of the ass, who was ignorant of this transaction, shared the feast, and joined in the chorus sung by the others, "The ass is gone, the ass is gone," without attaching any sense to the words, and blindly following their example. Next morning he asked his servant what had become of the ass, and the servant told him it had been sold, adding that he thought he had known it overnight, because he had heard him singing "The ass is gone" along with the other Sufis. In the course of this story there occur anecdotes of God consulting with the angels as to the creation of man, of a king who lost his hawk and found it again in the house of a poor old man, and of Shaikh Ahmad Khizrawiya buying sweetmeats for his

creditors.
Why the poet veils his doctrines in fables.
What is it hinders me from expounding my doctrines
But this, that my hearers' hearts incline elsewhere.
Their thoughts are intent on that Sufi guest;
They are immersed in his affairs neck deep.
So I am compelled to turn from my discourse
To that story, and to set forth his condition.
But, O friend, think not this Sufi a mere outward form,
As children see in a vine nothing but raisins.
O son, our bodies are as dried grapes and raisins;
If you are a man, cast away these things.
If you pass on to the pure mysteries of God,
You will be exalted above the nine heavenly spheres.
Now hear the outward form of my story,
But yet separate the grain from the chaff.
Why the prophets were sent.
God sent the prophets for this purpose,
Namely, to sever infidelity from faith.
God sent the prophets to mankind
That they might gather the pure grain on their tray.
Infidel and faithful, Mosalman and Jew,
Before the prophets came, seemed all as one.
Before they came we were all alike,
No one knew whether he was right or wrong.
Genuine coin and base coin were current alike;
The world was a night, and we travelers in the dark,
Till the sun of the prophets arose, and cried,
"Begone. O slumber; welcome, O pure light!"
Now the eye sees how to distinguish colors,
It sees the difference between rubies and pebbles.
The eye distinguishes jewels from dust,
Hence it is dust makes the eyes smart.
Makers of base coin hate the daylight,
Coins of pure gold love the daylight,

Because daylight is the mirror that reflects them,
So that they see their own perfect beauty.
Mystical Meaning of "Daylight"

God has named the resurrection "that day;"
Day shows off the beauty of red and yellow.
Wherefore "Day" in 'truth is the mystery of the saints;
One day of their moons is as whole years.
Know, "Day " is the reflection of the mystery of the saints,
Eye-closing night that of their hidden secrets.
Therefore hath God revealed the chapter "Daylight," 1
Which daylight is the light of the heart of Mustafa.
On the other view, that daylight means "The Friend,"
It is also a reflection of the same prophet.
For, as it is wrong to swear by a transitory being,
How can we suppose a transitory being spoken of by God?
The Friend of God said, "I love not them that set?" 2
How, then, could Allah have meant a transitory being?
Again, the words "by the night" mean Muhammad's veiling,
Namely, the fair earthly body that he bore;
When his sun proceeded from heaven on high
Into that body's night, it said, "He hath not forsaken thee;"
Union with God arose out of the depth of that disgrace;
That boon was the word, "He hath not been displeased."
Expressions of religious or other feeling derive their only
value from the state of mind from which they proceed.
Every expression is the sign of a state of mind;
That state is a hand, the expression an instrument.
A goldsmith's instruments in the hand of a cobbler
Are as grains of wheat sown on sand.
The tools of a cobbler in the hand of a cultivator

Are as grass before a dog or bones before an ass.
The words, "I am the Truth" were light in Mansur's 3
mouth,
In the mouth of Pharaoh "I am Lord Supreme" was
blasphemy.
The staff in the hand of Moses was a witness,
In the hands of the magicians it was naught.
For this cause 'Isa taught not to that foolish man
The words of power whereby he raised the dead.
For he who is ignorant misuses the instrument ;
If you strike flint on mud you will get no fire.
Hand and instrument resemble flint and steel;
You must have a pair; a pair is needed to generate.
He who has no peer or member is the "One,"
An uneven number, One without dispute!
Whoso says "one" and "two," and so on,
Confesses thereby the existence of the "One."
When the illusion of seeing double is swept away,
They who say "one" and "two" are even as they who say
"One."
If you take "One" as your ball in his tennis-field,
It is made to revolve by the strokes of his bat. 4
Yea, the ball that is even and without fault
Is made to revolve by the strokes of the King's hand.
O man of double vision, 5 hearken with attention,
Seek a cure for your defective sight by listening.
Many are the holy words that find no entrance
Into blind hearts, but they enter hearts full of light.
But the deceits of Satan enter crooked hearts,
Even as crooked shoes fit crooked feet.
Though you repeat pious expressions again and again,
If you are a fool, they affect you not at all;
Nay, not though you set them down in writing,
And though you proclaim them vauntingly;
Wisdom averts its face from you, O man of sin,

Wisdom breaks away from you and takes to flight!
0n Taqlid, blind imitation or cant.
"O wretch, why did you not come and say to me,
'Such and such a disastrous affair has occurred?'"
The servant replied, "By Allah, I came again and again,
That I might acquaint you with the matter.
You were always saying, 'The ass is gone, my lad!'
Along with the others in high excitement;
So I went away, thinking you knew all about it,
And were pleased at the transaction, being a wise man."
The Sufi said, "They were all singing the same words,
So I felt impelled to sing them as well.
Blind imitation of them has undone me.
Cursed be that blind imitation!"
The effect of blindly imitating unprofitable conduct
Is that men cast away honor for a morsel of bread.
The ecstasy of that company cast a reflection,
Whereby that Sufi's heart became ecstatic like them.
You need many reflections from your associates
In order to draw water from the peerless Ocean.
The first reflection cast is mere blind imitation;
After it has been often repeated you may test its truth.
Till it is thus verified, take it not from your friends;
The drop, not yet become pearl, sever not from its shell.
Evil influence of covetousness.

Would you have eyes and ears of reason clear,
Tear off the obstructing veil of greed!
The blind imitation of that Sufi proceeded from greed;
Greed closed his mind to the pure light.
Yea, 'twas greed that led astray that Sufi,
And brought him to loss of property and ruin.

Greed of victuals, greed of that ecstatic singing
Hindered his wits from grasping the truth.
If greed stained the face of a mirror,
That mirror would be as deceitful as we men are. 6
If a pair of scales were greedy of riches,
Would they tell truly the weight of anything?
The Prophet saith, "O people, through singleness of mind,
I ask of you no recompense for my prophesying; 7
I am a guide; God buyeth my guidance for you,
God giveth you my guidance in both worlds.
True, a guide deserves his wages;
Wages are due to him for directing you aright.
But what are my wages? The vision of The Friend.
Abu Bakr indeed offered me forty thousand pieces of
gold,But his forty thousand pieces were no wages for me.
How could I take brass beads for pearls of Aden?"
I will tell you a tale; hearken attentively,
That you may know how greed closes up the ears.
Every man subject to greed is a miser.
Can eyes of hearts clouded with greed see clearly?
The illusion of rank and riches blinds his sight,
Like hair dropping down before his eyes.
*NOTES:
1. Koran xciii: "By the daylight and by the night thy, Lord
hath not forsaken thee nor been displeased."
2. Koran vi. 76: "And when the night overshadowed
Abraham, he beheld a star, and he said, 'This is my Lord;'
but when it set he said, 'I love not Gods which set.'"
3. Mansur Hallaj, a celebrated Sufi who was put to death at
Bagdad in 309 A.H. for using these words.
4. i.e., unity is made to appear as plurality (see Gulshan i
Raz, I. 710).
5. See Gulshan i Raz, I. 104.
6. The Turkish commentator translates thus. The Lucknow
copy reads Ba sati for Ma sti.

7. Koran xi 53.

8. Abu Bakr made over all his goods to the Prophet in aid of the expedition to Syria.

STORY II.

The Pauper and the Prisoners.
A certain pauper obtained admittance to a prison, and
annoyed the prisoners by eating up all their victuals and
leaving them none. At last they made a formal complaint to
the Qazi, and prayed him to banish the greedy pauper from
the prison. The Qazi summoned the pauper before him, and
asked him why he did not go to his own house instead of
living on the prisoners. The pauper replied that he had no
house or means of livelihood except that supplied by the
prison; whereupon the Qazi ordered him to be carried
through the city, and proclamation to be made that he was a
pauper, that no one might be induced to lend him money or
trade with him. Accordingly the attendants sought for a
camel whereon to carry him through the city, and at last
induced a Kurd who sold firewood to lend his camel for the
purpose. The Kurd consented from greed of reward, and the
pauper, being seated on the camel, was carried through the
city from morning till evening, proclamation being made in
Persian, Arabic, and Kurdish that he was a pauper. When
evening came the Kurd demanded payment, but the pauper
refused to give him anything, observing that if he had kept
his ears open he must have heard the proclamation. Thus
the Kurd was led by greed to spend the day in useless labor.
Satan's office in the world.
The pauper said, "Your beneficence is my sustenance;
To me, as to aliens, your prison is a paradise.
If you banish me from your prison in reprobation,
I must needs die of poverty and affliction."
Just so Iblis said to Allah, "O have compassion;
Lord! respite me till the day of resurrection;
For in this prison of the world I am at oase,

That I may slay the children of my enemies.
From every one who has true faith for food,
And as bread for his provisions by the way,
I take it away by fraud or deceit,
So that they raise bitter cries of regret.
Sometimes I menace them with poverty, 2
Sometimes I blind their eyes with tresses and moles."
In this prison the food of true faith is scarce,
And by the tricks of this dog what there is is lost.
In spite of prayers and fasts and endless pains,
Our food is altogether devoured by him.
Let us seek refuge with Allah from Satan.
Alas ! we are perishing by his insolence.
The dog is one, yet he enters a thousand forms; 3
Whatever he enters straight becomes himself.
Whatever makes you shiver, know he is in it,
The Devil is hidden beneath its outward form.
When he finds no form at hand, he enters your thoughts,
To cause them to draw you into sin.
From your thoughts proceeds destruction,
When from time to time evil thoughts occur to you.
Sometimes thoughts of pleasure, sometimes of business,
Sometimes thoughts of science, sometimes of house and home.
Sometimes thoughts of gain and traffic,
Sometimes thoughts of merchandise and wealth.
Sometimes thoughts of money and wives and children,
Sometimes thoughts of wisdom or of sadness.
Sometimes thoughts of household goods and fine linen,
Sometimes thoughts of carpets, sometimes of sweepers.
Sometimes thoughts of mills, gardens, and villas,
Sometimes of clouds and mists and jokes and jests.
Sometimes thoughts of peace and war,
Sometimes thoughts of honor and disgrace.
Ah! cast out of your head these vain imaginations,

Ah! sweep out of your heart these evil suggestions.
Cry, "There is no power nor strength but in God!"
To avert the Evil One from the world and your own soul.
It is the true Beloved who causes all
outward earthly beauty to exist.
Whatsoever is perceived by sense He annuls,
But He establishes that which is hidden from the senses.
The lover's love is visible, his Beloved hidden.
The Friend is absent, the distraction he causes present.
Renounce these affections for outward forms,
Love depends not on outward form or face.
Whatever is beloved is not a mere empty form,
Whether your beloved be of the earth or of heaven.
Whatever be the form you have fallen in love with,
Why do you forsake it the moment life leaves it?
The form is still there; whence, then, this disgust at it?
Ah! lover, consider well what is really your beloved.
If a thing perceived by outward senses is the beloved,
Then all who retain their senses must still love it;
And since love increases constancy,
How can constancy fail while form abides? 4
But the truth is, the sun's beams strike the wall,
And the wall only reflects that borrowed light.
Why give your heart to mere stones, O simpleton?
Go! seek the source of light which shineth always!
Distinguish well true dawn from false dawn,
Distinguish the color of the wine from that of the cup;
So that, instead of many eyes of caprice,
One eye may be opened through patience and constancy.
Then you will behold true colors instead of false,
And precious jewels in lieu of stones.
But what is a jewel? Nay, you will be an ocean of pearls;
Yea, a sun that measures the heavens!
The real Workman is hidden in His workshop,
Go you into that workshop and see Him face to face.

Inasmuch as over that Workman His work spreads a curtain,
You cannot see Him outside His work.
Since His workshop is the abode of the Wise One,
Whoso seeks Him without is ignorant of Him.
Come, then, into His workshop, which is Not-being, 5
That you may see the Creator and creation at once.
Whoso has seen how bright is the workshop
Sees how obscure is the outside of that shop.
Rebellious Pharaoh set his face towards Being (egoism),
And was perforce blind to that workshop.
Perforce he looked for the Divine decree to change,
And hoped to turn his destiny from his door.
While destiny at the impotence of that crafty one
All the while was secretly mocking.
He slew a hundred thousand guiltless babes
That the ordinance and decree of Allah might be thwarted.
That the prophet Moses might not be born alive,
He committed a thousand murders in the land.
He did all this, yet Moses was born,
And was protected against his wrath.
Had he but seen the Eternal workshop,
He had refrained hand and foot from these vain devices.
Within his house was Moses safe and sound,
While he was killing the babes outside to no purpose.
Just so the slave of lusts who pampers his body
Fancies that some other man bears him ill-will;
Saying this one is my enemy, and this one my foe,
While it is his own body which is his enemy and foe,
He is like Pharaoh, and his body is like Moses,
He runs abroad crying, "where is my foe?"
While lust is in his house, which is his body,
He bites his finger in spite against strangers.
Then follows an anecdote of a man who slew his mother
because she was always misconducting herself with

14

strangers, and who excused himself by pleading that if he had not done so he would have been obliged to slay strangers every day, and thus incur blood-guiltiness. Lust is likened to this abandoned mother; when it is once slain, you are at peace with all men. In answer to an objection that if this were so the prophets and saints, who have subdued lust, would not have been hated and oppressed as they were, it is pointed out that they who hated the prophets in reality hated themselves, just as sick men quarrel with the physician or boys with the teacher. Prophets and saints are created to test the dispositions of men, that the good may be severed from the bad. The numerous grades of prophets, of saints, and of holy men are ordained, as so many curtains of the light of God, to tone down its brilliance, and make it visible to all grades of human sight.
*NOTES:
1. Koran vii. 13.
2. Koran ii. 279.
3. cf. Gulshan i Raz, p. 86.
4. This couplet exercises both the Turkish and the Lucknow commentators.
5. i.e., annihilation of self and of all phenomenal being, regarding self as naught in the presence of the Deity.

STORY III.

The King and his Two Slaves.
A king purchased two slaves, one extremely handsome, and the other very ugly. He sent the first away to the bath, and in his absence questioned the other. He told him that the first slave had given a very bad account of him, saying that he was a thief and a bad character, and asked if it was true. The second slave replied that the first was everything that was good, his inward qualities corresponding to the beauty of his outward appearance, and that whatever he had told the king was worthy of credit. The king replied that beauty was only an accident, and that, according to the tradition, accidents "endure only two moments;" that at death the animal soul is destroyed, that the text, "Whoso shall present himself with beauty shall receive tenfold reward," I does not refer to outward accidents, but to the "substance," the eternal soul. The slave in reply urged that the accidents of good works and thoughts will in some way bear fruit in the next world, pointing out that thought is always the precursor of the completed work, as the plan of the architect precedes the building, and the gardener's design the perfect fruit resulting from his labors. He added that the world is only the realized thought of "Universal Reason" 2 The king then sent away the slave with whom he had held this discourse, and summoned the other, and told him that his fellow slave had given a bad account of him, and asked what he had to say. He replied that his fellow slave was a liar and a rascal, and the king then dismissed him, observing that, in accordance with the tradition, "Every man is hidden under his own tongue," his tongue had betrayed his inner vileness. "The safety of a man lies in holding his tongue."
The apostolical succession of the prophets and the saints.

With that "brightness of lightning" 3 He kindled their souls
So that Adam acquired knowledge from that light.
That, which shone from Adam was gathered by Seth,
Wherefore Adam made him his viceroy when he saw it.
When Noah received the gift of that lustre,
He became a soul bearing pearls in the tempest of the flood.
By that light the soul of Abraham was led,
Without fear he entered Nimrod's fiery furnace.
When Ishmael sought out that light,
He meekly laid his head beneath his father's bright knife.
The soul of David was warmed by its heat,
Iron became pliable by the force of his weaving. 4
When Solomon was nurtured by its fruition,
The devils became the submissive slaves of his will.
When Jacob bowed his head to the Divine decree,
He recovered his sight at the scent of his son. 5
When moonlike Joseph saw that brilliant sun,
He became so expert as he was in interpreting dreams.
When the staff drew might from the hand of Moses,
It devoured the realm of Pharaoh at a mouthful.
When the soul of Jirjis 6 became privy to its light,
He sacrificed his life seven times, and regained it.
When Zakhariah 7 boasted of his love for it,
He ransomed his life in the hollow of the tree.
When Jonah swallowed a draught from that cup,
He found repose in the belly of the fish.
When John the Baptist became filled with its unction,
He laid his head in the golden charger in ardour for it.
When Jethro became aware of this exaltation,
He risked his life to find it.
Patient Job gave thanks for seven years,
For in his calamities he saw signs of its approach.

When Khizr and Elias boasted of gaining it,
They found the water of life and were no more seen.
When Jesus. Son of Mary, found that ladder of ascent,
He ascended to the height of the fourth heaven.
When Muhammad gained that blessed possession,
In a moment he cleft asunder the disk of the moon. 8
When Abu Bakr became the exemplar of that grace,
He was companion of that Lord, and a 'c faithful witness."
When 'Omar was enraptured with that beauty,
Like a mind he discerned true and false. 9
When Osman viewed those brilliant sights,
He diffused light and became "Lord of the two lights." 10
When Martaza ('Ali) shined with its reflection,
He became the "Lion of God" in the soul's domain.
When his two sons were illumined by this light,
They became the "pearly earrings of highest heaven;"
One of them losing his life by poison,
The other losing his head as he went about his march.
When Junaid was succoured by the forces of that light,
His ecstatic states exceeded counting.
Bayazid saw his way to increased fruition thereof,
And gained from God the name "Polestar of Gnostics."
What time King Mansur became victorious, 12
He left his throne and hastened to the stake.
When Karkhi of Karkh became its keeper,
He became lord of love and of the breath of Jesus.
Ibrahim son of Adham rode his horse to that point,
And became king of kings of equity.
And that Shakik starting from that junction
Became a sun of wit and acute of genius.
Fazil from a highway robber became a sage of the way, 13
When he was regarded with esteem by the King.
To Bishr Hafi the doctrine, was announced,
And he set his face towards the desert of inquiry.
When Zu-1-Ntin became distraught with care for it,

Egypt (Milk) as sugar became the house of his soul.
When Sari 14 lost his head in seeking the way thereto,
His rank was exalted above the seats of the mighty.
A hundred thousand great (spiritual) kings
Exalted by this divine light approach the world.
Their names remain hidden through God's jealousy;
Every beggar tells not their names. 15

*NOTES:

1. Koran vi. 161.
2. i.e., the Logos as Demiurge.
3. Koran xxiv. 43. The prophetic inspiration is likened to a light handed on from one to another.
4. Koran xxi. 80.
5. Koran lxxvii. 96.
6. Jirjis or St. George is supposed by Muhammadans to be the same person as Khizr or Elias.
7. Zakhariah the prophet is said to have taken refuge from his persecutors in the hollow of a tree.
8. Koran liv. 1.
9. Omar was called "The Discerner."
10. He bore this name because he had two daughters of Muhammad as his wives.
11. A tradition gives this title to Hasan and Hussain.
12. Mansur Hallaj, the celebrated Sufi impaled at Bagdad. Shah or King was a title often assumed by darveshes.
13. The "way" means the Sufi doctrines.
14. All these saints lived in the second and third centuries of the Flight.
15. In the introduction to the Nafahatu-'l Uns, Jami says there are always 4000 saints on the earth who are not even known to one another.

STORY IV.

The Falcon and the Owls.
A certain falcon lost his way, and found himself in the
waste places inhabited by owls. The owls suspected that he
had come to seize their nests, and all surrounded him to
make an end of him. The falcon assured them that he had
no such design as they imputed to him, that his abode was
on the wrist of the king, and that he did not envy their foul
habitation. The owls replied that he was trying to deceive
them, inasmuch as such a strange bird as he could not be a
favorite of the king. The falcon repeated that he was indeed
a favorite of the king, and that the king would assuredly
destroy their houses if they injured him, and proceeded to
give them some good advice on the folly of trusting to
outward appearances. He said, "It is true I am not
homogeneous with the king, but yet the king's light is
reflected in me, as water becomes homogeneous with earth
in plants. I am, as it were, the dust beneath the king's feet;
and if you become like me in this respect, you will be
exalted as I am. Copy the outward form you behold in me,
and perchance you will reach the real substance of the
king."
The right use of forms.
That my outward form may not mislead you,
Digest my sweet advice before copying me.
Many are they who have been captured by form,
Who aimed at form, and found Allah.
After all, soul is linked to body,
Though it in nowise resembles the body.
The power of the light of the eye is mated with fat,
The light of the heart is hidden in a drop of blood.
Joy harbors in the kidneys and pain in the liver,
The lamp of reason in the brains of the head;

Smell in the nostrils and speech in the tongue,
Concupiscence in the flesh and courage in the heart.
These connections are not without a why and a how,
But reason is at a loss to understand the how.
Universal Soul had connection with Partial Soul, 1
Which thence conceived a pearl and retained it in its bosom.
From that connection, like Mary,
Soul became pregnant of a fair Messiah;
Not that Messiah who walked upon earth and water,
But that Messiah who is higher than space. 2
Next, as Soul became pregnant by the Soul of souls,
So by the former Soul did the world become pregnant;
Then the World brought forth another world,
And of this last are brought forth other worlds.
Should I reckon them in my speech till the last day
I should fail to tell the total of these resurrections. 3
*NOTES:
1. This is a figurative account of the emanations of Absolute Being, whereby the world of phenomena is constituted (see Gulshan i Raz, p. 21, note, and p. 66).
2. i.e., the spirit of the Prophet Muhammad, whom the Sufis identify with the Primal Soul.
3. Continually is creation born again in a new creation" (Gulshan i Raz, p. 66). By constant effluxes from Absolute Being the world of phenomena is every moment renewed.

STORY V.

The Thirsty Man who threw Bricks into the Water.
A thirsty man discovered a tank of water, but could not
drink of it because it was surrounded by a high wall. He
took some of the bricks off the top of the wall and cast
them over it into the water. The water cried out, "What
advantage do you gain by doing this?" He made answer,
"The first advantage is this, that I hear your voice; and the
second, that the more bricks I pull off the wall, the nearer I
approach to you." The moral is, that so long as the wall of
the body intervenes, we cannot reach the water of life. The
abasement of the body brings men nearer to union with the
Deity. Destroy, therefore, the fleshly lusts which war
against the soul. Then follows another parable to illustrate
the folly of procrastination in this important matter.
"It was not ye who shot, but God shot; and
those arrows were God's not yours". 1
'Tis God's light that illumines the senses' light,
That is the meaning of "Light upon light." 2
The senses' light draws us earthwards,
God's light carries us heavenwards.
As objects of sense are of base condition,
God's light is an ocean, and the senses' light a dewdrop.
But that light which is "upon this light" is not seen,
Save through signs and holy discourses.
Since the senses' light is gross and dense,
It lies hidden in the black pupil of the eye.
When you cannot see the senses' light with the eye,
How can you see with the eye the Light of the mind?
As the senses' light is hidden in these gross veils,

22

Must not that Light which is pure be also hidden?
Like the senses, this world is ruled by a hidden Power.
It confesses its impotence before that hidden Power,
Which sometimes exalts it and sometimes lays it low,
Sometimes makes it dry and sometimes moist.
The hand is hidden, yet we see the pen writing;
The horse is galloping, yet the rider is hid from view.
The arrow speeds forth, yet the bow is not seen;
Souls are seen, the Soul of souls (God) is hidden.
Break not the arrow, for it is the arrow of the King
Yea, it is an arrow from the bow of Wisdom.
"Ye shot not when ye shot," was said by God;
God's action has predominance over all actions.
Break your own passion, break not that arrow,
The eye of passion takes milk to be blood.
Kiss that arrow and bear it to the King,
Yea, though it be stained with your own blood.
Whatsoever is seen is weak and base and impotent;
What is hidden is equally fierce and headstrong.
We are the captured game; who is the snare?
We are the balls; where is the bat?
He tears and mends; who is this tailor?
He fans and kindles the flame; who is this kindler?
At one time He makes the faithful one an infidel,
At another He makes the atheist a devotee!
Next comes an anecdote of a dirty man who refused to
bathe because he was ashamed to go into the water, with
the moral that "Shame hinders religion;" 3 and then another
of Zu'l Nun, a celebrated Egyptian Sufi of the third century
A.H. Zu'l Nun appeared to his ignorant friends to be mad,
and they accordingly confined him in a madhouse. After a
time they thought that he was not really mad, but had
feigned madness for some deep purpose, and they went to
the madhouse to inquire into the state of his health. When
they arrived there, Zu'l Nun asked them who they were, and

they answered that they were his devoted friends, who were now convinced that the story of his being mad was a calumny. Zu'l Nun jumped up and drove them away with sticks and stones, saying that true friendship would have been manifested in sharing his troubles, even as pure gold is tried by fire.

*NOTES:

1. Koran viii. 17, meaning, "God is the Fa'il i Hakiki, or Only Real Agent."

2. Koran xxiv. 35.

3. Freytag, Arabum Proverbia, vol. ii. pp. 379 and 418, gives two proverbs - one, "Shame is a part of religion;" and the other, "Shame hinders getting a livelihood."

STORY VI.

Luqman's Master examines him and discovers his Acuteness.

Luqman the Sage, 1 who is sometimes identified with Esop, and sometimes with the nephew of the prophet. Job, though "gifted with wisdom by God," was a slave. His master, however, discovered his worth, and became extremely attached to him, so that he never received any delicacy without giving Luqman a share of it. One day, having received a watermelon, he gave Luqman the best part of it, and Luqman devoured it with such apparent relish that his master was tempted to taste it. To his surprise he found it very bitter, and asked Luqman why he had not told him of this. Luqman replied that it was not for him, who lived on his master's bounty, to complain if he now and then received disagreeable things at his hands. Thus, though to outward appearance a slave, Luqman showed himself to be a lord.

Love endures hardships at the hands of the Beloved.
Through love bitter things seem sweet,
Through love bits of copper are made gold.
Through love dregs taste like pure wine,
Through love pains are as healing balms.
Through love thorns become roses,
And through love vinegar becomes sweet wine.
Through love the stake becomes a throne,
Through love reverse of fortune seems good fortune.
Through love a prison seems a rose bower,
Without love a grate full of ashes seems a garden.
Through love burning fire is pleasing light,
Through love the Devil becomes a Houri.
Through love hard stones become soft as butter,

Without love soft wax becomes hard iron.
Through love grief is as joy,
Through love Ghouls turn into angels.
Through love stings are as honey,
Through love lions are harmless as mice.
Through love sickness is health,
Through love wrath is as mercy.
Through love the dead rise to life,
Through love the king becomes a slave.
Even when an evil befalls you, have due regard;
Regard well him who does you this ill turn.
The sight which regards the ebb and flow of good and ill
Opens a passage for you from misfortune to happiness.
Thence you see the one state moves you into the other, 2
One opposite state generating its opposite in exchange.
So long as you experience not fears after joys,
How can you look for pleasures after disgusts?
While ye fear the doom of the angel on the left hand,
Men hope for the bliss of the angel on the right. 3
May you gain two wings! 4 A fowl with only one wing
Is impotent to fly, O well-intentioned one!
Now either permit me to hold my peace altogether,
Or give me leave to explain the whole matter.
And if you dislike this and forbid that,
Who can tell what your desire is?
You must have the soul of Abraham in order with light
To see the mansions of Paradise in the fire.
Step by step he ascended above sun and moon,
And so lagged not below, as a ring that fastens a door.
Since the "Friend of God" ascended above the heavens,
And said, "I love not Gods that set;" 5
So this world of the body is a breeder of misconceptions
In all who have not fled from lust.
*NOTES:
1. See Koran xxxi. Another anecdote of his wit occurs in

Book I.

2. The doctrine of Heraclitus, that opposite states generate one another, is discussed by Jelaludin in a passage quoted in Lumsden's Grammar, ii. 323, and is mentioned in the Phado and the Nicomachean Ethics.

3. An anacoluthon (see Koran i. 16).

4. The two wings are hope and fear, both of which are needed to guide men's religious flight (see Book III. on "Probability the guide of life").

5. Koran vi. 77.

STORY VII.

Moses and the Shepherd.

Next follows an anecdote of Bilkis, Queen of Sheba, whose reason was enlightened by the counsels of the Hoopoo sent to her by King Solomon. Outward sense is as opposed to true reason as Abu Jahl was to Muhammad; and when the outward senses are replaced by the true inner reason, man sees that the body is only foam, and the heart the limitless ocean. Afterwards comes an anecdote of a philosopher who was struck blind for cavilling at the verse, "What think ye? If at early morn your waters shall have sunk away, who will then give you clear running water?" 1 This is succeeded by the story of Moses and the shepherd. Moses once heard a shepherd praying as follows: "O God, show me where thou art, that I may become. Thy servant. I will clean Thy shoes and comb Thy hair, and sew Thy clothes, and fetch Thee milk." When Moses heard him praying in this senseless manner, he rebuked him, saying, "O foolish one, though your father was a Mosalman, you have become an infidel. God is a Spirit, and needs not such gross ministrations as, in your ignorance, you suppose." The shepherd was abashed at his rebuke, and tore his clothes and fled away into the desert. Then a voice from heaven was heard, saying, "O Moses, wherefore have you driven away my servant? Your office is to reconcile my people with me, not to drive them away from me. I have given to each race different usages and forms of praising and adoring me. I have no need of their praises, being exalted above all such needs. I regard not the words that are spoken, but the heart that offers them. I do not require fine words, but a burning heart. Men's ways of showing devotion to me are various, but so long as the devotions are genuine, they are

accepted."
Religious forms indifferent.
A voice came from God to Moses,
"Why hast thou sent my servant away?
Thou hast come to draw men to union with me,
Not to drive them far away from me.
So far as possible, engage not in dissevering;
'The thing most repugnant to me is divorce.' 2
To each person have I allotted peculiar forms,
To each have I given particular usages.
What is praiseworthy in thee is blameable in him,
What is poison for thee is honey for him.
What is good in him is bad in thee,
What is fair in him is repulsive in thee.
I am exempt from all purity and impurity,
I need not the laziness or alacrity of my people.
I created not men to gain a profit from them,
But to shower my beneficence upon them.
In the men of Hind the usages of Hind are praiseworthy,
In the men of Sind those of Sind.
I am not purified by their praises,
'Tis they who become pure and shining thereby.
I regard not the outside and the words,
I regard the inside and the state of heart.
I look at the heart if it be humble,
Though the words may be the reverse of humble.
Because the heart is substance, and words accidents,
Accidents are only a means, substance is the final cause.
How long wilt thou dwell on words and superficialities?
A burning heart is what I want; consort with burning!
Kindle in thy heart the flame of love,
And burn up utterly thoughts and fine expressions.
O Moses! the lovers of fair rites are one class,
They whose hearts and souls burn with love are another.
Lovers must burn every moment,

As tax and tithe are levied on a ruined village.
If they speak amiss, call them not sinners;
If a martyr be stained with blood, wash it not away.
Blood is better than water for martyrs,
This fault is better than a thousand correct forms.
No need to turn to the Ka'ba when one is in it,
And divers have no need of shoes.
One does not take a drunken man as a guide on the way,
Nor speak of darns to torn garments.
The sect of lovers is distinct from all others,
Lovers have a religion and a faith of their own.
Though the ruby has no stamp, what matters it?
Love is fearless in the midst of the sea of fear.
Beware, if thou offerest praises or thanksgivings,
And know them to be even as the babble of that shepherd;
Though thy praises be better compared with his,
Yet in regard to God they are full of defects.
How long wilt thou say, 'They obscure the truth,
For it is not such as they fancy'?
Thy own prayers are accepted only through mercy,
They are suffered as the prayers of an impure woman.
If her prayers are made impure by the flow of blood,
Thine are stained with metaphors and similitudes.
Blood is impure, yet its stain is removed by water;
But that impurity of ignorance is more lasting,
Seeing that without the blessed water of God
It is not banished from the man who is subject to it.
O that thou wouldst turn thy face to thy own prayers,
And become cognizant of the meaning of thy ejaculations,
And say, 'Ah! my prayers are as defective as my being;
O requite me good for evil!'"
Moses questions God as to the reason of
the flourishing state of the wicked.
Moses said, "O beneficent Creator,
With whom a moment's remembrance is as long ages,

I see Thy plan distorted in this world of earth and water;
My heart, like the angel's, feels a difficulty thereat.
With what object hast thou framed this plan,
And sowed therein the seeds of evil?
Why hast Thou kindled the fire of violence and wrong?
Why burnt up mosques and them who worship therein?
Paradise is attached to requirements unpleasant to us,
Hell is attached to things flattering our lusts.
The branch full of sap is the main fuel of thy fire.
'They that are burnt with fire are near to Kausar.' 3
Whoso is in prison and acquainted with troubles,
That is in requital for his gluttony and lusts.
Whoso is in a palace and enjoying wealth,
That is in reward for toils and troubles.
Whoso is seen enjoying uncounted gold and silver,
Know that he strove patiently to acquire it.
He, whose soul is exempt from natural conditions,
And who possesses the power of overriding causes,
Can see without causes, like eyes that pierce night;
But thou, who art dependent on sense attend to causes.
Having left Jesus, thou cherishest an ass (lust),
And art perforce excluded, like an ass;
The portion of Jesus is knowledge and wisdom,
Not so the portion of an ass, O asinine one!
Thou pitiest thine ass when it complains;
So art thou ignorant, thy ass makes thee asinine.
Keep thy pity for Jesus, not for the ass,
Make not thy lust to vanquish thy reason.
Leave thy natural lusts to whine and howl,
Tear thee from them, escape that snare of the soul!
*NOTES:
1. Koran lxvii. 30.
2. A tradition.
3. A saying of the Prophet.

STORY VIII.

The Man who made a Pet of a Bear. 1
A kind man, seeing a serpent overcoming a bear, went to
the bear's assistance, and delivered him from the serpent.
The bear was so sensible of the kindness the man had done
him that he followed him about wherever he went, and
became his faithful slave, guarding him from everything
that might annoy him. One day the man was lying asleep,
and the bear, according to his custom, was sitting by him
and driving off the flies. The flies became so persistent in
their annoyances that the bear lost patience, and seizing the
largest stone he could find, dashed it at them in order to
crush them utterly; but unfortunately the flies escaped, and
the stone lighted upon the sleeper's face and crushed it. The
moral is, "Do not make friends with fools." In the course of
this story occur anecdotes of a blind man, of Moses
rebuking the worshippers of the calf, and of the Greek
physician Galen and a madman.
He who needs mercy finds it.
Doing kindness is the game and quarry of good men,
A good man seeks in the world only pains to cure.
Wherever there is a pain there goes the remedy,
Wherever there is poverty there goes relief.
Seek not water, only show you are thirsty,
That water may spring up all around you.
That you may hear the words, "The Lord gives them to
drink," 2
Be athirst! Allah knows what is best for you.
Seek you the water of mercy? Be downcast,
And straightway drink the wine of mercy to intoxication.
Mercy is called down by mercy to the last.
Withhold not, then, mercy from any one, O son!
If of yourself you cannot journey to the Ka'ba,

Represent your helplessness to the Reliever.
Cries and groans are a powerful means,
And the All-Merciful is a mighty nurse.
The nurse and the mother keep excusing themselves,
Till their child begins to cry.
In you too has God created infant needs;
When they cry out, their milk is brought to them;
God said, "Call on God;" continue crying,
So that the milk of His love may boil up. 3
Moses and the worshipper of the calf.
Moses said to one of those full of vain imaginations,
"O malevolent one, through error and heresy
You entertain a hundred doubts as to my prophethood,
Notwithstanding these proofs, and my holy character.
You have seen thousands of miracles done by me,
Yet they only multiply your doubts and cavils.
Through doubts and evil thoughts you are in a strait,
You speak despitefully of my prophethood.
I brought the host out of the Red Sea before all men,
That ye might escape the oppression of the Egyptians.
For forty years meat and drink came from heaven,
And water sprang from the rock at my prayer.
My staff became a mighty serpent in my hand,
Water became blood for my ill-conditioned enemy.
The staff became a snake, and my hand bright as the sun;
From the reflection of that light the sun became a star.
Have not these incidents, and hundreds more like them,
Banished these doubts from you, O cold-hearted one?
The calf lowed through magic,
And you bowed down to it, saying, 'Thou art my God.' 4
The golden calf lowed; but what did it say,
That the fools should feel all this devotion to it?
You have seen many more wondrous works done by me,
But where is the base man who accepts the truth?
What is it that charms vain men but vanity?

What else pleases the foolish but folly?
Because each kind is charmed by its own kind,
Does a cow ever seek the lion?
Did the wolf show love to Joseph, 5
Or only fraud upon fraud with a view to devour him?
True, if it lose his wolf-like nature it becomes a friend;
Even as the dog of the cave became a son of man. 6
When good Abu Bakr saw Muhammad,
He recognized his truth, saying, 'This one is true;'
When Abu Bakr caught the perfume of Muhammad,
He said, 'This is no false one.'
But Abu Jahl, who was not one of the sympathizers,
Saw the moon split asunder, yet believed not.
If from a sympathizer, to whom it is well known,
I withhold the truth, still 'tis not hidden from him;
But he who is ignorant and without sympathy,
However much I show him the truth, he sees it not.
The mirror of the heart must needs be polished
Before you can distinguish fair and foul therein."
*NOTES:
1. Anwari Suhaili, i. 27.
2. Koran lxxvi. 21.
3. Koran xvii. 110.
4. See Koran xx. 90.
5. Koran xii. 17.
6. Koran xviii. 17.

STORY IX.

The Gardener and the Three Friends.
A voice came from heaven to Moses, saying, "O Moses
why didst thou not visit me when I was sick?" Moses
inquired the meaning of this dark saying, and the answer

was, "When one of God's saints is sick, God regards his sickness as His own; and, therefore, he who desires to hold companionship with God must not forsake the saints." 1 This is illustrated by a story of a gardener who saw three friends walking in his garden, and making free with his fruit. Knowing he could not prevail against them while they remained united, he contrived by tricks to separate them, and then proceeded to chastise them one by one. And this caused one of them to make the reflection that he had acted very foolishly in deserting his friends.

*NOTES:

1. Cp. Matthew xxv. 40.

STORY X.

Bayazid and the Saint.
The celebrated Sufi, Abu Yazid or Bayazid of Bastam, in
Khorasan, who lived in the third century of the Flight, was
once making a pilgrimage to Mecca, and visiting all the
"Pillars of insight" who lived m the various towns that lay
on his route. At last he discovered the "Khizr of the age" in
the person of a venerable Darvesh, with whom he held the
following conversation:
The Sage said, "Whither are you going, O Bayazid?
Where will you bring your caravan to a halt?"
Bayazid replied, "At dawn I start for the Ka'ba."
Quoth the Sage, "What provision for the way have you?"
He answered, "I have two hundred silver dirhams;
See them tied up tightly in the corner of my cloak."
The Sage said, "Circumambulate me seven times;
Count this better than circumambulating the Ka'ba;
And as for the dirhams, give them to me, O liberal one,
And know you have finished your course and obtained your
wish,
You have made the pilgrimage and gained the life to come,
You have become pure, and that in a moment of time.
Of a truth that is God which your soul sees in me,
For God has chosen me to be His house.
Though the Ka'ba is the house of His grace and favors,
Yet my body too is the house of His secret.
Since He made that house He has never entered it,
But none but That Living One enters this house;
When you have seen me you have seen God,
And have circumambulated the veritable Ka'ba.
To serve me is to worship and praise God;
Think not that God is distinct from me.

Open clear eyes and look upon me,
That you may behold the light of God in a mortal.
Tho Beloved once called the Ka'ba 'My house,'
But has said to me 'O my servant' seventy times;
O Bayazid, you have found the Ka'ba,
You have found a hundred precious blessings."
Bayazid gave heed to these deep sayings,
And placed them as golden earrings in his ears.
Then follow anecdotes of the Prophet paying a visit to one
of his disciples who lay sick, of Shaikh Bahlol, nicknamed
"The Madman," who was a favorite at the court of Harunu-
'r-Rashid, and of the people of Moses.
The sweet uses of adversity.

The sick man said, "Sickness has brought me this boon.
That this Prince (Muhammad) has come to me this morn,
So that health and strength may return to me
From the visit of this unparalleled King.
O blessed pain and sickness and fever!
O welcome weariness and sleeplessness by night!
Lo! God of His bounty and favor
Has sent me this pain and sickness in my old age;
He has given me pain in the back, that I may not fail
To spring up out of my sleep at midnight;
That I may not sleep all night like the cattle,
God in His mercy has sent me these pains.
At my broken state the pity of kings has boiled up,
And hell is put to silence by their threats!"
Pain is a treasure, for it contains mercies;
The kernel is soft when the rind is scraped off.
O brother, the place of darkness and cold
Is the fountain of life and the cup of ecstasy.

So also is endurance of pain and sickness and disease.
For from abasement proceeds exaltation.
The spring seasons are hidden in the autumns,
And autumns are charged with springs; flee them not.
Consort with grief and put up with sadness,
Seek long life in your own death!
Since 'tis bad, whatever lust says on this matter
Heed it not, its business is opposition.
But act contrary thereto, for the prophets
Have laid this injunction upon the world. 2
Though it is right to take counsel in affairs,
That you may have less to regret in the upshot;
The prophets have labored much
To make the world revolve on this pivot stone; 3
But, in order to destroy the people, lust desires
To make them go astray and lose their heads;
The people say, 'With whom shall we take counsel?'
The prophets answer, 'With the reason of your chief.'
Again they say, 'Suppose a child or a woman enter,
Who lacks reason and clear judgment; '
They reply, 'Take counsel with them,
And act contrary to what they advise.'
Know your lust to be woman, and worse than woman;
Woman is partial evil, lust universal evil.
If you take counsel with your lust,
See you act contrary to what that base one advises.
Even though it enjoin prayers and fasting,
It is treacherously laying a snare for you.'
You must abandon and ignore your own knowledge,
And dip your hand in the dish of abnegation of knowledge.
Whatever seems profitable, flee from it,
Drink poison and spill the water of life.
Contemn whatever praises you,
Lend to paupers your wealth and profits!
Quit your sect and be a subject of aversion,

Cast away name and fame and seek disgrace!"
God the Author of good and evil.
If you seek the explanation of God's love and favor,
In connection therewith read the chapter "Brightness." 4
And if you say evil also proceeds from Him,
Yet what damage is that to His perfection?
To send that evil is one of His perfections.
I will give you an illustration, O arrogant one;
The heavenly Artist paints His pictures of two sorts,
Fair pictures and pictures the reverse of fair.
Joseph he painted fair and made him beautiful;
He also painted ugly pictures of demons and 'afrits.
Both sorts of pictures are of His workmanship,
They proceed not from His imperfection, but His skill,
That the perfection of His wisdom may be shown,
And the gainsayers of His art be put to shame.
Could He not paint ugly things He would lack art,
And therefore He creates Guebers as well as Moslems.
Thus, both infidelity and faith bear witness to Him,
Both alike bow down before His almighty sway.
But know, the faithful worship Him willingly,
For they seek and aim at pleasing Him;
While Guebers worship Him unwillingly,
Their real aim and purpose being quite otherwise.
Evil itself is turned into good for the good.
The Prophet said to that sick man,
"Pray in this wise and allay your difficulties;
'Give us good in the house of our present world,
And give us good in the house of our next world. 5
Make our path pleasant as a garden,
And be Thou, O Holy One, our goal!'"
The faithful will say on the last day, "O King!
Was not Hell on the route all of us traveled?
Did not faithful as well as infidels pass through it?
Yet on our way we perceived not the smoke of the fire;

Nay, it seemed Paradise and the mansion of the blessed."
Then the King will answer, "That green garden,
As it appeared to you on your passage through it,
Was indeed Hell and the place of dread torment;
Yet for you it became a garden green with trees.
Since you have labored to make hellish lusts,
And the 'fire of pride that courts destruction,
To make these, I say, pure and clean,
And, to please God, have quenched those fires,
So that the fire of lust, that erst breathed flame,
Has become a holy garden and a guiding light,
Since you have turned the fire of wrath to meekness,
And the darkness of ignorance to shining knowledge,
Since you have turned the fire of greed into bounty,
And the vile thorns of malice into a rose-garden;
Since you have quenched all these fires of your own
For my sake, so that those poisons are now pure sweets;
Since you have made fiery lust as a verdant garden,
And have sowed therein the seed of fidelity,
So that nightingales of prayer and praise
Ever warble sweetly around this garden;
Since you have responded to the call of God,
And have drawn water out of the hell of lust,
For this cause my hell also, for your behoof,
Becomes a verdant garden and yields leaves and fruit."
What is the recompense of well-doing, O son?
It is kindness and good treatment and rich requital.
Have ye not said, "We are victims,
Mere nothings before eternal Being?
If we are drunkards or madmen,
'Tis that Cup-bearer and that Cup which make us so.
We bow down our heads before His edict and ordinance,
We stake precious life to gain His favor.
While the thought of the Beloved fills our hearts,
All our work is to do Him service and spend life for Him.

Wherever He kindles His destructive torch,
Myriads of lovers' souls are burnt therewith.
The lovers who dwell within the sanctuary
Are moths burnt with the torch of the Beloved's face."
O heart haste thither, 6 for God will shine upon you,
And seem to you a sweet garden instead of a terror.
He will infuse into your soul a new soul,
So as to fill you, like a goblet, with wine.
Take up your abode in His soul!
Take up your abode in heaven, O bright full moon!
Like the heavenly Scribe,7 He will open your heart's book
That He may reveal mysteries unto you.
Abide with your Friend, since you have gone astray,
Strive to be a full moon; you are now a fragment thereof.
Wherefore this shrinking of the part from its whole?
Why this association with its foes?
Behold Genus become Species in due course,
Behold secrets become manifest through his light!
So long as woman-like you swallow blandishments,
How, O wise man, can you get relief from false flatteries?
These flatteries and fair words and deceits (of lust)
You take, and swallow, just like women.
But the reproaches and the blows of Darveshes
Are really better for you than the praises of sinners.
Take the light blows of Darveshes, not the honey of
sinners,
And become, by the fortune of good, good yourself.
Because from them the robe of good fortune is gained,
In the asylum of the spirit blood becomes life.
*NOTES:
1. Alluding to the Hadis: "Heaven and earth contain me
not, but the heart of my faithful servant contains me."
2. Freytag quotes a saying of 'Omar, "A fool may indicate
the right course" (Arabum Proverbia, i. p. 566).
3. The law defining the right course.

4. Koran xciii. : "By the noonday brightness, and by the night when it darkeneth, thy Lord hath not forsaken thee nor been displeased."
5. "O Lord, give us good in this world and good in the next, and save us from the torment of the fire." (Koran ii. 197).
6. i.e., to annihilation of self in God, as a moth in the flame.
7. Atarid or Mercury.

STORY XI.

Mo'avia and Iblis.

Mo'avia, the first of the Ommiad Khalifas, was one day
lying asleep in his palace, when he was awakened by a
strange man. Mo'avia asked him who he was, and he
replied that he was Iblis. Mo'avia then asked him why he
had awakened him, and lblis replied that the hour of prayer
was come, and he feared Mo'avia would be late. Mo'avia
answered, "Nay! it could never have been your intention to
direct me in the right way. How can I trust a thief like you
to guard my interests?" Iblis answered, "Remember that I
was bred up as an angel of light, and that I cannot quite
abandon my original occupation. You may travel to Rome
or Cathay, but still you retain the love of your fatherland. I
still retain my love of God, who fed me when I was young;
nay, even though I revolted from Him, that was only from
jealousy (of Adam), and jealousy proceeds from love, not
from denial of God. I played a game of chess with God at
His own desire, and though I was utterly checkmated and
ruined, in my ruin I still experience God's blessings."
Mo'avia answered, "What you say is not credible. Your
words are like the decoy calls of a fowler, which resemble
the voices of the birds, and so lure them to destruction. You
have caused the destruction of hundreds of mortals, such as
the people of Noah, the tribe of 'Ad, 1 the family of Lot,
Nimrod, Pharaoh, Abu Jahl, and so on."
Iblis retorted, "You are mistaken if you suppose me to be
the cause of all the evil you mention. I am not God, that I
should be able to make good evil, or fair foul. Mercy and
vengeance are twin divine attributes, and they generate the

43

good and evil seen in all earthly things. I am, therefore, not to blame for the existence of evil, as I am only a mirror, which reflects the good and evil existing in the objects presented to it."

Mo'avia then prayed to God to guard him against the sophistries of Iblis, and again adjured Iblis to cease his arguments and tell plainly the reason why he had awakened him. Iblis, instead of answering, continued to justify himself, saying how hard it was that men and women should blame him when they did anything wrong, instead of blaming their own evil lusts. Mo'avia, in reply, reproached him with concealing the truth, and ultimately brought him to confess that the true reason why he had awakened him was this, that if he had overslept himself, and so missed the hour of prayer, he would have felt deep sorrow and have heaved many sighs, and each of these sighs would, in the sight of God, have counted for as many as two hundred ordinary prayers.

The value of sighs.

A certain man was going into the mosque,
Just as another was coming out.
He inquired of him what had occurred to the meeting,
That the people were coming out of the mosque so soon.
The other told him that the Prophet
Had concluded the public prayers and mysteries.
"Whither go you," said he, "O foolish one,
Seeing the Prophet has already given the blessing?"
The first heaved a sigh, and its smoke ascended;
That sigh yielded a perfume of his heart's blood.
The other, who came from the mosque, said to him,
"Give me that sigh, and take my prayers instead."
The first said, "I give it, and take your prayers."
The other took that sigh with a hundred thanks.
He went his way with deep humility and contrition,
As a hawk who had ascended in the track of the falcon.

44

That night, as ho lay asleep, he heard a voice from heaven,
"Thou hast bought the water of life and healing;
The worth of what thou hast chosen and possessed
Equals that of all the people's accepted prayers."
To illustrate the treachery of wolves in sheep's clothing, -
of Satans rebuking sin and preaching religion - an anecdote
is told of a master of a house who caught a thief, but was
induced to let him escape by the stratagem of the thief's
confederate, who cried that he had got the real thief
elsewhere. Apropos of the same theme, the poet next
relates the story of "those who built a mosque for
mischief," as recorded in the Koran. 2 The tribe of Bani
Ganim built a mosque, and invited the Prophet to dedicate
it. The Prophet, however, discovered that their real motive
was jealousy of the tribe of Bani Amru lbn Auf, and of the
mosque at Kuba, near Medina, and a treacherous
understanding with the Syrian monk Abu Amir, and
therefore he refused their request, and ordered the mosque
to be razed to the ground.
Wisdom the believer's lost camel.
My people adopt my law without obeying it,
They take that coin without assaying it.
The Koran's wisdom is like the "believer's lost camel,' 3
Every one is certain his camel is lost.
You have lost your camel and seek it diligently;
Yet how will you find it if you know not your own?
What was lost? Was it a female camel that you lost?
It escaped from your hand, and you are in a maze.
The caravan is come to be loaded,
Your camel is vanished from the midst of it.
You run here and there, your mouth parched with heat;
The caravan moves on, and night approaches.
Your goods lie on the ground in a dangerous road,
You hurry after your camel in all directions.
You cry "O Moslems, who has seen a camel,

Which escaped from its stable this morning?
To him who shall give me news of my camel
I will give a reward of so many dirhems."
You go on seeking news of your camel from every one,
And every lewd fellow flatters you with a fresh rumor,
Saying, "I saw a camel; it went this way;
'Twas red, and it went towards this pasture."
Another says, "Its ear was cropped."
Another says, "Its cloth was embroidered."
Another that it had only one eye,
Another that it had lost its hair from mange.
To gain the reward every base fellow
Mentions a hundred marks without any foundation.
All false doctrines contain an element of truth.
Just so every one in matters of doctrine
Gives a different description of the hidden subject.
A philosopher expounds it in one way,
And a critic at once refutes his propositions.
A third censures both of them;
A fourth spends his life in traducing the others.
Every one mentions indications of this road,
In order to create an impression that he has gone it.
This truth and that truth cannot be all true,
And yet all of them are not entirely astray in error.
Because error occurs not without some truth,
Fools buy base coins from their likeness to real coins.
If there were no genuine coins current in the world,
How could coiners succeed in passing false coins?
If there were no truth, how could falsehood exist?
Falsehood derives its plausibility from truth.
'Tis the desire of right that makes men buy wrong;
Let poison be mixed with sugar, and they eat it at once.
If wheat were not valued as sweet and good for food,
The cheat who shows wheat and sells barley would make
no profit!

Say not, then, that all these creeds are false,
The false ones ensnare hearts by the scent of truth.
Say not that they are all erroneous fancies,
There is no fancy in the universe without some truth.
Truth is the "night of power " 4 hidden amongst other nights,
In order to try the spirit of every night.
Not every night is that of power, O youth,
Nor yet is every night quite void of power.
In the crowd of rag-wearers there is but one Faqir; 5
Search well and find out that true one.
Tell the wary and discerning believer
To distinguish the king from the beggar.
If there were no bad goods in the world,
Every fool might be a skilful merchant;
For then the hard art of judging goods would be easy.
If there were no faults, one man could judge as well as another.
Again, if all were faulty, skill would be profitless.
If all wood were common, there would be no aloes.
He who accepts everything as true is a fool,
But he who says all is false is a knave.
*NOTES:
1. See Koran xi. 63.
2. Koran ix. 108.
3. This is a proverb ascribed to Ali. It means, people are always losing wisdom and seeking it like a lost camel (Freytag, Arabum Proverbia, i. p. 385).
4. The night on which the Koran was revealed.
5. So in the Phaedo, "Many are the wandbearers, but few the Mystics."

STORY XII.

The Four Hindustanis who censured one another.
Four Hindustanis went to the mosque to say their prayers.
Each one duly pronounced the Takbir, and was saying his
prayers with great devotion, when the Mu'azzin happened
to come in. One of them immediately called out, "O
Mu'azzin, have you yet called to prayer? It is time to do
so." Then the second said to the speaker, "Ah! you have
spoken words unconnected with worship, and therefore,
according to the Hadis, you have spoiled your prayers." 1
Thereupon the third scolded the last speaker, saying, "O
simpleton, why do you rebuke him? Rather rebuke
yourself." Last of all, the fourth said, "God be praised that I
have not fallen into the same ditch as my three
companions." The moral is, not to find fault with others,
but rather, according to the proverb, 2 to be admonished by
their bad example. Apropos of this proverb, a story is told
of two prisoners captured by the tribe of Ghuz. The
Ghuzians were about to put one of them to death, to
frighten the other, and make him confess where the treasure
was concealed, when the doomed man discovered their
object, and said, "O noble sirs, kill my companion, and
frighten me instead."
*NOTES:
1. Mishkat ul Masabih, by Matthews, i. 205.
2. Freytag, Arabum Proverbia, i. 628.

STORY XIII.

The Old Man and the Physician.
An old man complained to his physician that he suffered
from headache. The physician replied, "That is caused by
old age." The old man next complained of a defect in his
sight, and the physician again told him that his malady was
due to old age. The old man went on to say that he suffered
from pain in the back, from dyspepsia, from shortness of
breath, from nervous debility, from inability to walk, and so
on; and the physician replied that each of these ailments
was likewise caused by old age. The old man, losing
patience, said, "O fool, know you not that God has ordained
a remedy for every malady?" The physician answered,
"This passion and choler are also symptoms of old age.
Since all your members are weak, you have lost the power
of self-control, and fly into a passion at every word."
Bad principles always produce bad acts.
Fools laud and magnify the mosque,
While they strive to oppress holy men of heart.
But the former is mere form, the latter spirit and truth.
The only true mosque is that in the hearts of saints.
The mosque that is built in the hearts of the saints
Is the place of worship of all, for God dwells there.
So long as the hearts of the saints are not afflicted,
God never destroys the nation.
Our forefathers lifted their hands against the prophets;
Seeing their bodies, they took them for ordinary men.
In you also abide the morals of those men of old;
How can you avoid fearing that you will act like them?
The morals of those unthankful ones dwell in you,
Your urn will not always return unbroken from the well.
Seeing that all these bad symptoms are seen in you,
And that you are one with those men, how can you escape?

STORY XIV.

The Arab Carrier and the Scholar.
An Arab loaded his camel with two sacks, filling one with wheat and the second with sand, in order to balance the first. As he was proceeding on his way he met a certain tradition-monger, who questioned him about the contents of his sacks. On learning that one contained nothing but sand, he pointed out that the object might be attained much better by putting half the wheat in one sack and half in the other. On hearing this, the Arab was so struck by his sagacity that he conceived a great respect for him, and mounted him on his camel. Then he said, "As you possess such great wisdom. I presume that you are a king or a Vazir, or at least a very rich and powerful noble." The theologian, replied, "On the contrary. I am a very poor man; all the riches my learning has brought me are weariness and headaches, and I know not where to look for a loaf of bread." The Arab said, "In that case get, off my camel and go your way, and suffer me to go mine, for I see your learning brings ill luck." The moral of the story is the worthlessness of mere human knowledge, and its inferiority to the divine knowledge proceeding from inspiration. This thesis is further illustrated by an account of the mighty works which were done by the saint Ibrahim bin Adham, through the divine knowledge that God had given him. Ibrahim was originally prince of Balkh, but renounced his kingdom and became a saint. One day he was sitting by the shore mending his cloak, when one of his former subjects passed by and marvelled to see him engaged in such a, mean occupation. The saint at once, by inspired knowledge, read his thoughts,

and thus corrected his false impressions. He took the needle with which he was mending, his cloak and cast it into the sea. Then with a loud voice he cried out, "O needle rise again from the midst of the sea and come back again into my hands." Without a moment's delay thousands of fishes rose to the surface of the sea, each bearing in its mouth a golden needle, and cried out, "O Shaikh, take these needles of God!" Ibrahim then turned to the noble, saying, "Is not the kingdom of the heart better than the contemptible earthly kingdom I formerly possessed? What you have just seen is a very trifling sign of my spiritual power as it were, a mere leaf plucked to show the beauty of a garden. You have now caught the scent of this garden, and it ought to attract your soul to the garden itself, for you must know that scents have great influence, e.g., the scent of Joseph's coat, 1 which restored Jacob's sight, and the scents which were loved by the Prophet." 2

*NOTES:

1. Koran xii. 93.

2. There is a Hedis: "The Prophet loved perfumes and fair women and brightness of eyes in prayer."

STORY XV.

The Man who boasted that God did not punish
him for his sins, and Jethro's answer to him.
That person said in the time of Shu'aib (Jethro),
"God has seen many faults done by me;
Yea, how many sins and faults of mine has He seen,
Nevertheless of His mercy He punishes me not."
God Almighty spake in the ear of Shu'aib,
Addressing him with an inner voice in answer thereto,
"Why hast thou said I have sinned so much,
And God of His mercy has not punished my sins?"
Thou sayest the very reverse of the truth, O fool!
Wandering from the way and lost in the desert!
How many times do I smite thee, and thou knowest not?
Thou art bound in my chains from head to foot.
On thy heart is rust on rust collected,
So thou art blind to mysteries.
Thy rust, layer on layer, O black kettle!
Makes the aspect of thy inner parts foul.
If that smoke touched a new kettle,
It would show the smut, were it only as a grain of barley;
For everything is made manifest by its opposite,
In contrast with its whiteness that black shows foul.
But when the kettle is black, then afterwards
Who can see on it the impression of the smoke?
If the blacksmith be a negro,
His face agrees in color with the smoke.
But if a man of Rum does blacksmith's work,
His face becomes grimed by the smoke fumes;
Then he quickly perceives the impression of his fault,

So that he wails and cries 'O Allah!'
When he is stubborn and follows his evil practices,
He casts dust in the eyes of his discernment.
He recks not of repentance, and, moreover, that sin
Becomes dear to his heart, so that he becomes without faith,
Old shame for sin and calling on God quit him,
Rust five layers deep settles on his mirror,
Rust spots begin to gnaw his iron,
The color in his jewel grows less and less.
When you write on white paper,
What is written is read at a glance;
But when you write on the face of a written page,
It is not plain, reading it is deceptive;
For that black is written on the top of other black,
Both the writings are illegible and senseless.
Or if, in the third place, you write on the page,
And then blacken it like an infidel's soul,
Then what remedy but the aid of the Remedier?
Despair is copper and sight its elixir.
Lay your despair before Him,
That you may escape from pain without medicine."
When Shu'aib spoke these aphorisms to him,
From that breath of the soul roses bloomed in his heart,
His soul heard the revelations of heaven;
He said, "If He has punished me, where is the sign of it?"
Shu'aib said, "O Lord, he repels my arguments,
He seeks for a sign of that punishment."
The Veiler of sins replied, "I will tell him no secrets,
Save only one, in order to try him.
One sign that I punish him is this,
That he observes obedience and fasting and prayer,
And devotions and almsgiving, and so on,
Yet never feels the least expansion of soul.
He performs the devotions and acts enjoined by law,

Yet derives not an atom of relish from them.
Outward devotion is sweet to him, spirit is not sweet,
Nuts in plenty, but no kernel in any of them.
Relish is needed for devotions to bear fruit,
Kernels are needed that seeds may yield trees.
How can seeds without kernels become trees?
Form without soul (life) is only a dream."

STORY XVI.

The Gluttonous Sufi.
In a certain convent there lived a Sufi whose conduct gave
just offence to the brethren. They brought him before their
Shaikh and thus accused him, "This Sufi has three very bad
qualities; he babbles exceedingly like a bell, at his meals he
eats more than twenty men and when he sleeps he is as one
of the Seven Sleepers." The Shaikh then admonished him,
insisting on the obligation of keeping to the golden mean;
and reminding him that even the prophet Moses 1 was once
rebuked by Khizr for speaking to excess. But the delinquent
excused himself on the grounds that the mean is relative,
what is excess in one man being moderation in another, that
he who is led by the spirit is no longer subject to the
outward law, and that, the "inner voice," which rules such
an one s conduct, is its own evidence.
The mean is relative.

He said, "Though the path of the mean is wisdom,
Yet is this same mean also relative.
The water which is insufficient for a camel
Is like an ocean to a mouse.
Whoso has four loaves as his daily allowance,
Whether he eat two or three, he observes the mean.
But if he eat all four he transgresses the mean,
A very slave to greed, and voracious as a duck.
Whoso has an appetite for ten loaves,
Know, though he eat six, he observes the mean.
If I have an appetite for fifty loaves,
While you can manage only six, we are not on a par.

You are wearied with ten prostrations in prayer,
Whilst I can endure five hundred.
Such an one goes barefoot to the Ka'ba,
Whilst another faints with going to the mosque."
The ecstatic state which exalts the subject of it above law.
"At times my state resembles a dream,
My dreaming seems to them infidelity.
Know my eyes sleep, but my heart is awake;
My body, though torpid, is instinct with energy.
The Prophet said, 'Mine eyes sleep,
But my heart is awake with the Lord of mankind.'
Your eyes are awake and your heart fast asleep,
My eyes are closed, and my heart at the 'open door.'
My heart has other five senses of its own;
These senses of my heart view the two worlds.
Let not a weakling like you censure me,
What, seems night to you is broad day to me;
What seems a prison to you is a garden to me.
Busiest occupation is rest to me.
Your feet are in the mire, to me, mire is rose,
What to you is funeral wailing is marriage drum to me.
While I seem on earth, abiding with you in the house,
I ascend like Saturn to the seventh heaven.
'Tis not I who companion with you, 'tis my shadow;
My exaltation transcends your thoughts,
Because I have transcended thought,
Yea, I have sped beyond reach of thought.
I am lord of thought, not overlorded by thought,
As the builder is lord of the building.
All creatures are enslaved to thought;
For this cause are they sad at heart and sorrowful.
I send myself on an embassy to thought,
And, at will, spring back again from thought.
I am as the bird of heaven and thought as the fly,
How can the fly lend a helping hand to me?

Whoso has in him a spark of the light of Omnipotence,
However much he eats, say ' Eat on;' 'tis lawful to him."
To the spiritual man the "inner voice" is its
own evidence, and needs no other proof.
"If you are a true lover of my soul,
This truth-fraught saying of mine is no vain pretence,
'Though I talk half the night I am superior to you;'
And again, 'Fear not the night; here am I, your kinsman.'
These two assertions of mine will both seem true to you
The moment you recognize the voice of your kinsman.
Superiority and kinsmanship are both mere assertions,
Yet both are recognized for truth by men of clear wit.
The nearness of the voice proves to such an one
That the voice proceeds from a friend who is near.
The sweetness of the kinsman's voice, too, O beloved,
Proves the veracity of that kinsman.
But the uninspired fool who from ignorance
Cannot tell the voice of a stranger from a friend's,
To him the friend's saying seems a vain pretension,
His ignorance is the material cause of his disbelief.
To the wise, whose hearts are enlightened,
The mere sound of that voice proves its truth."
"When you say to a thirsty man, 'Come quickly;
This is water in the cup, take and drink it,'
Does the thirsty man say, 'This is a vain pretension;
Go, remove yourself from me, O vain pretender,
Or proceed to give proofs and evidence
That this is generic water, and concrete water thereof'?
Or when a mother cries to her sucking babe,
'Come, O son, I am thy mother,'
Does the babe answer, 'O mother, show a proof
That I shall find comfort from taking thy milk'?
In the hearts of every sect that has a taste of the truth
The sight and the voice of prophets work miracles.
When the prophets raise their cry to the outward ear,

The souls of each sect bow in devotion within;
Because never in this world hath the soul's ear
Heard from any man the like of that cry.
That poor man in that strange sweet voice
Recognizes the voice of God, 'Verily I am nigh.'" 2
*NOTES:
1. Koran xviii. 77.
2. "And when my servants ask thee concerning me then
will I be nigh unto them. I will answer the cry of him that
crieth, when he crieth unto me." (Koran ii. l82).

STORY XVII.

The Tree of Life.

The preceding story is followed by a short anecdote of the
infants of the Virgin Mary and the mother of John the
Baptist leaping in their mothers' wombs, 1 and in reply to
matter of fact cavillers and questioners of this anecdote, the
poet says we must look at its spirit and essential basis
rather than its outward form. This introduces the story of
the tree of life. A certain wise man related that in Hindustan
there was a tree of such wonderful virtue that whosoever
ate of its fruit lived forever. Hearing this, a king deputed
one of his courtiers to go in quest of it. The courtier
accordingly proceeded to Hindustan, and traveled all over
that country, inquiring of every one he met where this tree
was to be found. Some of these persons professed their
entire ignorance, others joked him, and others gave him
false information; and, finally, he had to return to his
country with his mission unaccomplished. He then, as a last
resource, betook himself to the sage who had first spoken
of the tree, and begged for further information about it, and
the sage replied to him as follows:
The Shaikh laughed, and said to him, "O friend,
This is the tree of knowledge, O knowing one;
Very high, very fine, very expansive,
The very water of life from the circumfluent ocean.
Thou hast run after form, O ill-informed one,
Wherefore thou lackest the fruit of the tree of substance.
Sometimes it is named tree, sometimes sun,
Sometimes lake, and sometimes cloud.
'Tis one, though it has thousands of manifestations;
Its least manifestation is eternal life!
Though 'tis one, it has a thousand manifestations,
The names that fit that one are countless.

That one is to thy personality a father,
In regard to another person He may be a son.
In relation to another He may be wrath and vengeance,
In relation to another, mercy and goodness.
He has thousands of names, yet is One,
Answering to all of His descriptions, yet indescribable.
Every one who seeks names, if he is a man of credulity,
Like thee, remains hopeless and frustrated of his aim.
Why cleavest thou to this mere name of tree,
So that thou art utterly balked and disappointed?
Pass over names and look to qualities,
So that qualities may lead thee to essence!
The differences of sects arise from His names;
When they pierce to His essence they find His peace!"
This story is followed by another anecdote illustrative of
the same thesis that attending merely to names and outward
forms, rather than to the spirit and essence of religion, leads
men into error and delusion. Four persons, a Persian, an
Arab, a Turk, and a Greek, were traveling together, and
received a present of a dirhem. The Persian said he would
buy "angur" with it, the Arab said he would buy "inab,"
while the Turk and the Greek were for buying "uzum" and
"astaphil" (staphyle), respectively. Now all these words
mean one and the same thing, viz. "grapes;" but, owing to
their ignorance of each other's languages, they fancied they
each wanted to buy something different, and accordingly a
violent quarrel arose between them. At last a wise man who
knew all their languages came up and explained to them
that they were all wishing for one and the same thing.

*NOTES:
1. Luke i. 41.

STORY XVIII.

The Young Ducks who were brought up under a Hen.
Although a domestic fowl may have taken thee,
Who art a duckling, under her wing and nurtured thee,
Thy mother was a duck of that ocean.
Thy nurse was earthy, and her wing dry land.
The longing for the ocean which fills thy heart,
That natural longing of thy soul comes from thy mother.
Thy longing for dry land comes to thee from thy nurse;
Quit thy nurse, for she will lead thee astray.
Leave thy nurse on the dry land and push on,
Enter the ocean of real Being, like the ducks!
Though thy nurse may frighten thee away from water,
Do thou fear not, but haste on into the ocean!
Thou art a duck, and flourishest on land and water,
And dost not, like a domestic fowl, dig up the house.
Thou art a king of "the sons of Adam honored by God," 1
And settest foot alike on sea and land;
For impress on thy mind, "We have carried them by sea,"
Before the words, "We have carried them by land."
The angels go not on dry land,
And the animals know nothing of the sea;
Thou in body art an animal, in thy soul an angel;
Hence thou goest both upon earth and on heaven."
Hence to outward view "He is a man like you," 2
While to his sharp-seeing heart "it hath been revealed."
His earthy form has fallen on earth,
His spirit revolving above highest heaven.
O boy, we are all of us waterfowl,
The sea knows full well our language.
Solomon 3 is, as it were, that sea, and we as the birds;

In Solomon we hold our course to eternity.
Along with Solomon plunge into the ocean, 4
Then, like David, the water will make us coats-of-mail.
That Solomon is present to every one,
But negligence closes their eyes and bewitches them.
Hence, through ignorance, sloth, and folly,
Though he stands hard by us, we are shut off from him.
The noise of thunder makes the head of the thirsty ache;
When he knows not that it unlocks the blessed showers,
His eyes are fixed on the running stream,
Unwitting of the sweetness of the rain from heaven.
He urges the steed of his desire towards the caused,
And perforce remains shut off from the Causer.
Whoso beholds the Causer face to face,
How can he set his heart on things caused on earth?

End of the book.